NBA CHAMPIONSHIPS:

↓

NONE

↓

ALL-TIME LEADING SCORER:

↓

DELL CURRY (1988–98):

↓

9,839 POINTS

THE NBA: A HISTORY OF HOOPS

CHARLOTTE HORNETS

BY JIM WHITING

CREATIVE EDUCATION   CREATIVE PAPERBACKS

Published by Creative Education
and Creative Paperbacks

P.O. Box 227, Mankato, Minnesota 56002

Creative Education and Creative Paperbacks
are imprints of The Creative Company

www.thecreativecompany.us

Design and production by Blue Design
Printed in the United States of America

Photographs by Alamy (Tribune Content Agency
LLC), AP Images (ASSOCIATED PRESS), Getty
Images (Lisa Blumenfeld/Getty Images Sport, Scott
Cunningham/NBA, Tim DeFrisco/Getty Images
Sport, Kevork Djansezian/Getty Images Sport, Mike
Ehrmann/Getty Images Sport, Fernando Medina/
NBA, Panoramic Images, Kent Smith/NBA), Newscom
(CHRIS KEANE 329/CHRIS KEANE/Icon SMI, DAVID T.
FOSTER III/MCT, Jim Middleton/UPI Photo Service,
Albert Pena/Cal Sport Media, Jeff Siner/ABACAUSA.
COM, Jeff Siner/MCT, Chris Szagola/Cal Sport Media)

Library of Congress Cataloging-in-Publication Data

Names: Whiting, Jim, 1943- author.

Title: Charlotte Hornets / Jim Whiting.

Series: The NBA: A History of Hoops.

Includes bibliographical references and index.

Summary: This high-interest title summarizes the
history of the Charlotte Hornets professional
basketball team, highlighting memorable events
and noteworthy players such as Larry Johnson.

Identifiers: LCCN 2016046223 / ISBN 978-1-
60818-838-3 (hardcover) / ISBN 978-1-62832-441-9
(pbk) / ISBN 978-1-56660-886-2 (eBook)

Subjects: LCSH: 1. Charlotte Hornets (Basketball team:
2014-)—History—Juvenile literature. 2. Charlotte
Hornets (Basketball team: 2014-)—Biography—
Juvenile literature. 3. Charlotte Bobcats (Basketball
Team)—History—Juvenile literature. 4. Charlotte
Hornets (Basketball team: 1988-2002)—History—
Juvenile literature. 5. Charlotte Hornets (Basketball
team: 1988-2002)—Biography—Juvenile literature.

Classification: LCC GV885.52.C4 W55 2017 /
DDC 796.323/640975676—dc23

CCSS: RI.4.1, 2, 3, 4; RI.5.1, 2, 4; RI.6.1, 2, 3;
RF.4.3, 4; RF.5.3, 4; RH. 6-8. 4, 5, 7

First Edition HC 9 8 7 6 5 4 3 2 1

First Edition PBK 9 8 7 6 5 4 3 2 1

CONTENTS

LEGENDS OF THE HARDWOOD

Named after a British monarch, **CHARLOTTE** is also called the "Queen City."

THE HORNETS
BEGIN TO BUZZ

The game was a perfect one to show on TV. The new Charlotte Hornets of the National Basketball Association (NBA) hosted the Chicago Bulls. It was December 23, 1988. Chicago's best player was

Michael Jordan. He had helped the nearby University of North Carolina win the 1982 college championship. In the basketball-crazy state, no one stood taller. This game gave local fans their first chance of seeing him in person as a professional. Everything seemed to favor the Bulls. The Hornets were a collection of unwanted veterans and untested rookies.

10

C harlotte had won just 7 of its first 24 games. But on this day, the crowd screamed as the score was tied 101–101 with seconds remaining. Hornets power forward Kurt Rambis shoved a teammate out of the way. He tipped the ball into the basket as time ran out. The Hornets won! "The place went nuts," Rambis said. "It went absolutely nuts." Team publicist Harold Kaufman added, "That was the birth of Hornets hysteria.... It wasn't just a sporting event. In terms of

Former NBA star **MICHAEL JORDAN** became majority owner of the team in 2010.

12

THE LITTLE CITY
THAT COULD

LEGENDS OF THE HARDWOOD

In 1985, the NBA said it would add four teams. Charlotte businessman George Shinn put together a group to make a bid. Ten other cities were interested. Many people thought the Charlotte area was too small to support a team. The owners voted the following year. A newspaper writer noted, "The only franchise Charlotte is going to get is one with golden arches." That was a reference to McDonald's. Shinn wasn't discouraged. "I had been on the bottom before," he said. "Keep your faith, keep pushing, keep believing." His presentation impressed the owners. Charlotte was the top choice for an NBA team.

something that transformed a city and a franchise and set it on a certain path, I think that one game did that more than anything else."

C

harlotte had received its franchise more than two years earlier. Owner George Shinn asked Charlotte city leaders to help him name the team. The Spirit, they suggested. "Look, you accomplished this goal against all odds," they said. "The spirit of this city, and your spirit, is what made this happen." No one else liked the name. One reporter wrote, "What's Shinn's mascot going to be, Casper the Friendly Ghost?" So Shinn asked for input from fans. The overwhelming choice was Hornets. The name dates back to the Revolutionary War. The British army came up against powerful fighters in the Charlotte area. A general wrote to King George III, "this place is like fighting in a hornet's nest." A local minor league baseball team was also the Hornets. A team in the short-lived World Football League had used the name, too.

Veteran guard **KELLY TRIPUCKA** scored the first points for the Hornets franchise.

15

Before they played a single game, the Hornets made their mark on the NBA. Famed fashion designer Alexander Julian used teal as the uniform color. No other sports team used it. Within a few years, teams at all levels wore teal. The Hornets were also the first NBA team to use pinstripes on their uniforms. It set a trend.

Unfortunately, the first game was unfashionably lopsided. The Hornets lost by 40 points to the Cleveland Cavaliers. They finished the year at 20–62. Small forward Kelly Tripucka averaged more than 22 points a game. He led the team in scoring. Guard Dell Curry provided instant offense off the bench.

ACCORDING TO PLAN

Despite the losing record, Charlotte led the league in attendance. One reason was fan favorite point guard Tyrone "Muggsy" Bogues. At 5-foot-3, he is still the shortest player in NBA history.

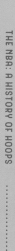

17

Versatile guard **KENDALL GILL** thrilled fans with his soaring slam dunks.

LARRY JOHNSON won Rookie of the Year honors in 1991–92.

Bogues joined the team in 1988 after his rookie season with the Washington Bullets. General manager Carl Scheer knew his team wouldn't top the league right away. His plan was to make the playoffs in five years. The team's second year wasn't any better. The team finished 19–63. The Hornets showed modest improvement in 1990–91 with a 26–56 mark. The next year, they drafted power forward Larry Johnson. He and second-year guard

LEGENDS OF THE HARDWOOD

MAYBE SIZE DOESN'T MATTER

MUGGSY BOGUES, POINT GUARD, 5-FOOT-3, 1988–97

When Muggsy was young, his friends thought he was too short to play basketball. In desperation, he used the bottoms of milk crates as baskets. He became a powerful defender. Finally, others saw his talent. He starred in high school and college. Despite his small stature, Bogues played in 14 NBA seasons. He notched 6,858 points (7.7 average), 6,726 assists (7.6 average), and 1,369 steals. Perhaps most remarkably, he blocked 39 shots. One block came against 7-footer Patrick Ewing on April 14, 1993. Ewing was about to go up for a dunk when Muggsy stripped the ball.

As a rookie, center **ALONZO MOURNING** blocked nine shots in two games.

Kendall Gill boosted the team. But a late-season slide resulted in a 31–51 record.

The team drafted center Alonzo Mourning before the 1992–93 season. "Most rookies are a little intimidated coming into this league," said coach Allan Bristow. "'Zo' never backs down from anybody." Johnson became the first Hornets player chosen for the NBA All-Star Game. The young talent carried Charlotte to its first winning season at 44–38. The Hornets were exactly on time with Scheer's plan. The Hornets brimmed with confidence in the playoffs. They defeated the favored Boston Celtics in the first round. But they bowed out in the Eastern Conference semifinals to the New York Knicks. The Hornets won just one of five games. Despite the loss, the Hornets seemed to be on the rise.

MOURNING and the Hornets faced Jordan's Bulls in the 1995 playoffs.

22

But the injury bug stung the Hornets. Both Mourning and Johnson missed large chunks of the following season. They returned to help the team finish 41–41. Both players were healthy for 1994–95, though. Mourning averaged 21 points and 10 rebounds a game. Both he and Johnson played in the All-Star Game. Charlotte won 50 games for the first time. But the defending NBA champion Chicago Bulls swatted them out of the first round of the playoffs.

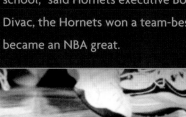

LEGENDS OF THE HARDWOOD

WORST DRAFT DECISION?

The Hornets took Kobe Bryant in the 1996 NBA Draft. Almost immediately, they traded him to the Los Angeles Lakers for center Vlade Divac. Was this a bad decision? Charlotte needed a proven center after trading Alonzo Mourning. The Lakers said they would trade Divac to the Hornets if they drafted Bryant. "Here was a 17-year-old kid [Bryant] who had played in high school," said Hornets executive Bob Bass. "We made a decision to win now and not later." With Divac, the Hornets won a team-best 54 games. He left after one more season. Bryant, of course, became an NBA great.

24

CONTINUED SUCCESS

The Hornets wanted to sign Mourning to a long-term contract. He didn't think the team offered enough money. So Charlotte traded him. One player they got in return was forward Glen Rice. He

Forward **GLEN RICE** led the Hornets in scoring during his three seasons with the team.

Big man **ELDEN CAMPBELL** gave the Hornets strength in scoring and rebounding.

"WE PLAYED HARD, BUT WE'VE STILL GOT A WAYS TO GO TO BE A CHAMPION."

played in the All-Star Game. But the Hornets went just 41–41. Charlotte rebounded in 1996–97 behind Rice's sharpshooting. He averaged nearly 27 points. It was the third best in the league. Charlotte went 54–28, the best record in its history. But again the Hornets couldn't get out of the first round, losing 3–0 to the Knicks.

Charlotte said goodbye to the popular Bogues the following season. Still, the team was almost as good as the previous year, winning 51 games. This time, the Hornets defeated the Atlanta Hawks in the first round of the playoffs. They fell to the Chicago Bulls in the conference semifinals. "We played hard, but we've still got a ways to go to be a champion," said coach Dave Cowens. A players' strike delayed the 1998–99 season. After that, Charlotte struggled. The team made yet another coaching change. Paul Silas replaced Cowens. As a player, Silas had a reputation as a tough rebounder and defender. He urged his

Tenacious defender **DAVID WESLEY** helped Charlotte to the playoffs four times.

28

players to take the same attitude. "Paul told us we could sit around and lick our wounds, or we could go out and make something of our season," said guard David Wesley. The team responded. A late run brought their record to 26–24, just short of the playoffs.

Charlotte barreled into the following season. It went 49–33 before losing to Philadelphia in the first round of the playoffs. The Hornets won 46 games in 2000–01 and 44 the following season. Both times they easily won the first round of the playoffs. The Hornets pushed the Milwaukee Bucks to a deciding Game 7 in the conference semifinals in 2001. But they lost 104–95. The following year, they lost the semifinals to the New Jersey Nets.

LEGENDS OF THE HARDWOOD

THE ART OF BLOCKING SHOTS

EMEKA OKAFOR, CENTER/POWER FORWARD, 6-FOOT-10, 2004–09

Emeka Okafor's first basketball skill was blocking shots. He averaged 7 blocks a game in high school and 4.3 in college. For most shots, he turned sideways so that he could reach his right arm as high as possible. He faced would-be dunkers straight on, though. This helped him absorb some of the other person's weight. Blocking shots is risky. The force of the ball can smash one's fingers against the rim or backboard. Despite the potential dangers, Okafor rejected 10 New York Knicks shots in a game on January 12, 2007. His favorite block? "They were all good," he replied. "I love all my children."

At 7-foot-2, Slovenian center **PRIMOZ BREZEC** often had the upper hand.

EXIT HORNETS, ENTER BOBCATS

Georg Shinn was a hero to the people of Charlotte at first. But by 2000, he had serious legal problems. Fans turned against him. He became even less popular when he demanded that the city

32

build a new arena at no cost to him. He said the team couldn't make enough money in the current space. The city refused. Shinn asked to move the team to New Orleans when the 2001–02 season ended. As part of the deal, the NBA promised Charlotte a new team. It would begin playing in 2004. The new team's owner was Robert Johnson.

The first order of business was naming the team. During a six-month process, three finalists emerged: Bobcats, Dragons, and Flight. As Johnson explained in his announcement of the winner, "No one wants to meet up with a bobcat in the woods, and that's the feeling we intend to create on the court with our team's new identity." There were other reasons for the nickname. The bobcat was a natural feline companion to the Carolina Panthers, the city's professional football team. Many people thought the nickname also referred to Johnson's first name.

Before the 2004–05 season, the Bobcats selected several players from other teams. New coach Bernie Bickerstaff knew his team wouldn't be a contender right away. He didn't want to spend money on older veterans. They would be gone after a couple of years. Instead, he focused on players such as forward Gerald Wallace. He had spent most of his three years with the Sacramento Kings on the bench. "We're a bunch of young guys who got overlooked," said Wallace, nicknamed "Crash" for his aggressive playing style. "All you want in this game is a

SAME CITY, NEW NAME

Like Charlotte and New Orleans, other pro teams have changed their names while staying in the same city. Such changes were very common in baseball. The most recent team to revise its name was Tampa Bay. They dropped the "Devil" from the "Rays" in 2008. In 1922, football's Chicago Staleys changed to the Bears. Pittsburgh renamed its football Pirates to Steelers in 1940. Long after the New York Titans became the Jets (1963), the Tennessee Oilers took on the Titans name (1999). For the NBA, the Denver Rockets became the Nuggets in 1974. The Washington Bullets became the Wizards in 1997.

chance to show that you can play. This is our chance." Charlotte also had the second overall pick of the 2004 NBA Draft. It took forward/center Emeka Okafor. "Emeka is a great player, but we see more than that in him," said Bickerstaff. "We are counting on his intelligence, strength, and maturity to pull this young team together." Okafor did his best. He was named Rookie of the Year. In November, Charlotte defeated the defending champion Detroit Pistons 91–89. It was the first time in 33 years an expansion team defeated the champions. The next month, Okafor drained two last-second free throws to beat New Orleans 94–93 in overtime. "The fans wanted us to beat the Hornets, and we sensed it meant a lot to the city," he said. Despite these highlights, the team struggled. It ended the season with an 18–64 record.

Nevertheless, opposing teams respected the young Bobcats' effort. "Everybody said Charlotte was crazy because they went with all kids," said Houston Rockets coach Jeff Van Gundy. "But those kids fear no one and play their hearts out. They are only going to get better." They did. Charlotte won 26 games the following season. Then the team added one of the game's all-time legends. Michael Jordan became a part-owner. He also served as manager of basketball operations. The team continued to improve. The Bobcats won 35 games in 2008–09.

36

THE HORNETS RETURN

The Bobcats traded Okafor to New Orleans before the 2009–10 season. They received another shot-blocker, 7-foot-1 center Tyson Chandler, in return. Charlotte added fiery guard Stephen Jackson in

Shot-blocking center **TYSON CHANDLER** tipped the Bobcats into the playoffs in 2010.

BORIS DIAW was known as "3D" for his ability to play multiple positions on the court.

"WHEN IT COMES TO BAD TEAMS, SOME CAN'T SCORE ... AND SOME CAN'T DEFEND.... THE BOBCATS CAN'T DO EITHER. THEY'RE THE LEAGUE'S WORST OFFENSIVE TEAM *AND* THE LEAGUE'S WORST DEFENSIVE TEAM."

November. The Bobcats clawed their way to a 44–38 record. But the Orlando Magic swept them in the first round. Johnson sold the team to Jordan. "Purchasing the Bobcats is the culmination of my post-playing career goal of becoming the majority owner of an NBA franchise," Jordan said. Charlotte stumbled to a 34–48 mark the following season.

T hen the bottom fell out. In the strike-shortened 2011–12 season, Charlotte won only 7 games while losing 59. Charlotte's .106 winning percentage was the worst in NBA history. As nba.com writer John Schuhmann noted, "When it comes to bad teams, some can't score ... and some can't defend.... The Bobcats can't do either. They're the league's worst offensive team *and* the league's worst defensive team, a double-dip that has been accomplished only two other times in the last 35 years."

40

HUGO THE HORNET

More than 6,000 people entered the team's "name the mascot" contest in 1988. Hugo the Hornet was the winner. Cheryl Henson designed his costume. She is the daughter of Muppets creator Jim Henson. Hugo stayed with the team when it moved to New Orleans. In 2013, Pierre the Pelican replaced him to reflect the change in the team's name. Hugo returned to Charlotte when the team became the Hornets again. Hugo is a four-time winner of the NBA Mascot Slam Dunk Championship. The *NBA Inside Stuff* TV show twice named him winner of the NBA Best Mascot Award.

LEGENDS OF THE HARDWOOD

Sharpshooting **KEMBA WALKER** averaged 20.9 points a game in 2015–16, breaking that career high in 2016–17.

he team's bad luck continued with the 2012 NBA Draft. In the lottery system, New Orleans beat out Charlotte for the top pick. The Hornets drafted future superstar Anthony Davis. Charlotte took defensive specialist small forward Michael Kidd-Gilchrist with the second pick. General manager Rich Cho said, "Out of the 17 years I've been in the NBA and involved with draft interviews and draft dinners, he's in the top five as far as that goes. Just a very, very high-character guy. Just a great, great work ethic, and he's only going to get better." Kidd-Gilchrist lived up to Cho's expectations. He was named to the

Elite defender **MICHAEL KIDD-GILCHRIST** worked to improve his offensive play.

42

From 2009 to 2015, guard **GERALD HENDERSON** was a consistent performer in Charlotte.

NBA All-Rookie second team. Charlotte also added veteran guard Ben Gordon. The new blood helped the Bobcats go 7–5 to open the 2012–13 season. But they soon had an 18-game losing streak and finished 21–61. New coach Steve Clifford helped Charlotte improve to 43–39 and return to the playoffs the following year. The powerful Miami Heat swept the Bobcats. "Clifford has transformed [Charlotte's] work environment, turning a wayward operation into competence," said sports writer Adrian Wojnarowski. "They have an identity—defense, rebounding, and relentless player development amid a challenged roster."

Veteran forward **MARVIN WILLIAMS** posted a career-high 10 double-doubles in 2015–16.

"TODAY IS TRULY AN HISTORIC DAY FOR OUR FRANCHISE, OUR CITY, AND OUR FANS AS WE MARK THE OFFICIAL RETURN OF THE CHARLOTTE HORNETS."

Soon, the Bobcats added to that character. The new owner of the New Orleans Hornets wanted to rename his team. He chose Pelicans. The brown pelican is Louisiana's state bird. Jordan asked the league to return the Hornets nickname to Charlotte. The league agreed. "Today is truly an historic day for our franchise, our city, and our fans as we mark the official return of the Charlotte Hornets," Jordan said. The NBA also returned the history of the original Hornets to Charlotte.

Key injuries and other factors limited the Hornets the following season. They finished at 33–49. However, hopes ran high for the 2015–16 season. Charlotte drafted 2015 College Player of the Year Frank Kaminsky and traded for small forward Nicolas Batum. Unfortunately, Kidd-Gilchrist injured his shoulder during a preseason game. He was ruled out for the entire season. Still, the Hornets enjoyed a winning record and a playoff berth. The Miami Heat bounced them out of the playoffs in the first round. With Kidd-Gilchrist healthy, Charlotte was poised for another playoff appearance in 2016–17. But the Hornets had won just 3 of 20 games by the time 7-foot center Cody Zeller was sidelined with injuries. They finished 36–46.

As Coach Clifford continued to develop his younger players, Charlotte fans kept buzzing with excitement for their team. They hoped that a championship banner would soon hang in Charlotte's Time Warner Cable Arena.

SELECTED BIBLIOGRAPHY

Ballard, Chris. *The Art of a Beautiful Game: The Thinking Fan's Tour of the NBA*. New York: Simon & Schuster, 2010.

Drape, Joe. *In the Hornets' Nest: Charlotte and Its First Year in the NBA*. New York: St. Martin's Press, 1989.

Hareas, John. *Ultimate Basketball: More Than 100 Years of the Sport's Evolution*. New York: DK, 2004.

Hubbard, Jan, ed. *The Official NBA Basketball Encyclopedia*. 3rd edition. New York: Doubleday, 2000.

NBA.com. "Charlotte Hornets." http://www.nba.com/hornets/.

Sports Illustrated. *Sports Illustrated Basketball's Greatest*. New York: Sports Illustrated, 2014.

WEBSITES

JR. NBA

http://jr.nba.com/

This kids site has games, videos, game results, team and player information, statistics, and more.

NO SMALL FEAT: THE NBA'S SHORTEST PLAYER NEVER GAVE UP

http://www.npr.org/2014/10/25/358358540/the-nbas-shortest-player
-never-gave-up

Read or listen to this inspiring story of Muggsy Bogues from National Public Radio.

Note: Every effort has been made to ensure that any websites listed above were active at the time of publication. However, because of the nature of the Internet, it is impossible to guarantee that these sites will remain active indefinitely or that their contents will not be altered.

INDEX